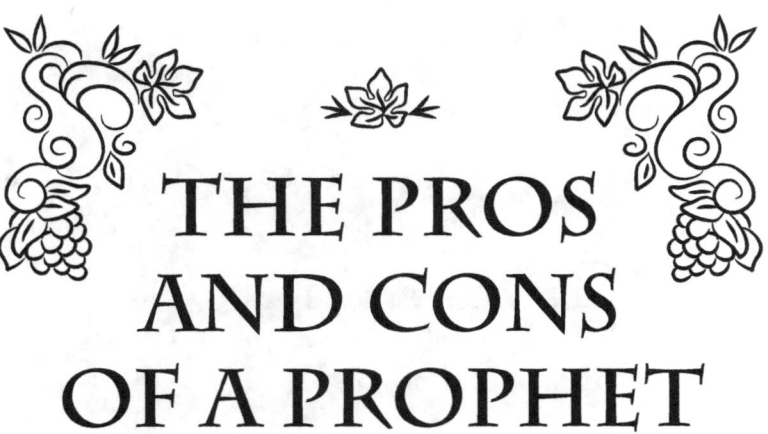

THE PROS
AND CONS
OF A PROPHET

The Mantle and The Mess of The Office

Apostle Paul B. Campbell Jr.

Copyright © 2023 Paul B. Campbell Jr.

All rights reserved. No part of this book may be reproduced in any form or by any electronic or mechanical means, including information storage and retrieval systems, without permission in writing from the publisher, except by reviewers, who may quote brief passages in a review.

ISBN: 978-1-955312-46-2

Printed in the United States of America

Story Corner Publishing & Consulting, Inc.

3810 Indian River Rd. Suite 13031

Chesapeake, VA 23325

Storycornerpublishing@yahoo.com
www.StoryCornerPublishing.com

— *Dedication* —

I dedicate this book to all the Prophets who want to live by God's ordinances.

TABLE OF CONTENTS

— Introduction —

Today, we have more encounters with Prophets than we can count. Sometimes we can point them out, and other times they go unnoticed. A true Prophet of the Lord is a blessing to encounter because it is an experience with God that can change your life. The prophet holds a governmental position in the body of Christ, and they speak on God's behalf. The prophet is an ambassador that represents God. I had many questions about prophets until I discovered I was one of them. God began to reveal Himself to me in ways I could not explain to the typical person. At first, I thought I was crazy when God spoke to me. Then it grew on me. God always instructed me to carry out an assignment when prophesying was far from my mind or I hesitated to speak. After a while, I knew God was working on my boldness and obedience. A prophet must be both because the enemy will use people to knock you down and have you second-guess God. I had to learn quickly because Satan doesn't play fair, and he longs for the day to wipe out the Lord's prophets! If he had it his way, we would all die because he only comes to steal, kill, and destroy. I thank God every day for being on my side. If God be for me, who can be against me?

I am handpicked and chosen by God. He loves me, and I love Him for that. Prophets, it's time to arise and declare the Kingdom of God with understanding! No one can teach you how to be a prophet except the Holy Spirit, but we all need help understanding what we see and hear. Most times, God will explain the answers to our questions, but other times God would send someone our way to release words of knowledge. Hence, why The School of The Prophets was formed in the Bible. In this book, you will learn the insight of a prophet's life, the "do's" and "don't" of the office the prophet holds, and maybe even figure out if you are a prophet of the Lord.

— Chapter 1 —

HISTORY OF THE PROPHET

"Before I formed you in the womb, I knew you, before you were born I set you apart; I appointed you as a prophet to the nations. "Alas, Sovereign Lord," I said, "I do not know how to speak; I am too young." But the Lord said to me, "Do not say, 'I am too young.' You must go to everyone I send you to and say whatever I command you. Do not be afraid of them, for I am with you and will rescue you," declares the Lord. Then the Lord reached out his hand and touched my mouth and said to me, "I have put my words in your mouth. See, today I appoint you over nations and kingdoms to uproot and tear down, to destroy and overthrow, to build and to plant." Jeremiah 1:5-10 NIV.

Jeremiah was a prophet of The Lord that heard instructions directly from God. The Lord appointed and affirmed him for his journey. Jeremiah's objective as a prophet was to uproot, tear down, destroy, overthrow, build, and plant spiritually and naturally. He was an agent hired by God to carry out his instructions. Yes, Jeremiah was young and lacked confidence, but don't we all at some point? That did not matter to God because He invested in Jeremiah, just as He does with all His prophets, and He expects a return. God also protects His investments because we are significant to Him. God handpicks prophets to speak on His behalf. God chooses His prophets even before they are formed in the womb. God sent Prophet Jeremiah to carry out his anointed ministry at an appointed time in his life. God creates, sanctifies, and anoints a prophet before birth, but a prophet does not immediately start their ministry at birth. God has appointed a time for each of His prophets to be activated and understand their calling. God will reveal to the prophet when it is time.

A prophet is an inspired teacher or proclaimer of the Will of God. A prophet (or seer) is one inspired by God through the Holy Spirit to deliver God's message. Prophets are God's messengers who speak God's truth to others. The English word *prophet* comes from the Greek word *prophetes*, meaning "one who speaks forth" or "advocate." Prophets have teaching and revelatory roles in releasing God's truth. Some are called "seers" because of their spiritual insight or ability to "see" the future and God's movements throughout the earth and spirit realm. Although not all prophets are seers, they can see at the appointed time what God chooses to release to them. For example, prophet Isaiah's ministry touched on the present and the future. He preached boldly against the corruption of his day.

> *"Woe to the sinful nation, a people whose guilt is great, a brood of evildoers, children given to corruption! They have forsaken the Lord; they have spurned the Holy One of Israel and turned their backs on him." Isaiah 1:4 NIV.*

Prophets will not consistently deliver a message everyone favors, but that does not cancel or change the assignment. Although prophets only see in part, they are commissioned to carry out all the instructions God releases to them. It's their mandate from God.

> *"For now, we see only a reflection as in a mirror; Then we shall see face to face. Now I know in part; then I shall know fully, even as I am fully known." 1 Corinthians 13:12 NIV.*

Prophets faithfully speak God's word to the people. They were even instrumental in guiding the nation of Israel and establishing the church in the Old Testament. The Lord builds the foundation of His household on the apostles and prophets. In most churches run by apostles, you will find a prophet assisting. Sometimes you will even find apostles that are prophets as well. Apostles are the builders, whereas prophets are the divine instructors.

"Consequently, you are no longer foreigners and strangers, but fellow citizens with God's people and also members of his household, built on the foundation of the apostles and prophets, with Christ Jesus himself as the chief cornerstone." Ephesians 2:19-20 NIV.

A congregation without a prophet is blind because God gives foresight to the seer. Understand if there is a seer among a people, they will preserve and prosper that people because of their anointed sight.

"This is why it says: When he ascended on high, he took many captives and gave gifts to his people. So Christ himself gave some apostles, some prophets, some evangelists, some pastors, and some teachers to equip his people for works of service so that the body of Christ may be built up until we all reach unity in the faith and in the knowledge of the Son of God and become mature, attaining to the whole measure of the fullness of Christ." Ephesians 4: 8,11-13 NIV.

The Types of Prophets

Prophet is a governmental position that helps govern the church. Only those chosen by Jesus/ Yeshua are prophets. They carry an authority to help manage Jesus's church. It is in their personality, thought process, outlook, etc., to think or act as a governing office holder. A prophet is in one's DNA because it's who they are created to be.

The office of a prophet equips the saints to do the work they are called to do (Ephesians 4:12), including helping them to maturity. That is much more involved work.
This position is only given by the head of the church, Jesus/Yeshua. We may ask for this position, but there are no guarantees He will choose us because prophets are appointed before birth.

The Godhead distributes different abilities, callings, and skills to each member of the body of Christ:
God the Father: Operations (or functions)

Lord Jesus Christ: Administrations (or offices)

Holy Spirit: Is prophecy

Operations from the Father

Romans 12:4-8 NIV, "For just as each of us has one body with many members, and these members do not all have the same function, so in Christ, we, though many, form one body, and each member belongs to all the others. We have different gifts according to the grace given to each of us. If your gift is prophesying, then prophesy in accordance with your faith; if it is serving, then serve; if it is teaching, then teach; if it is to encourage, then give encouragement; if it is giving, then give generously; if it is to lead, do it diligently; if it is to show mercy, do it cheerfully."

God assigned seven different functions to all members of the body of Christ, with one of these being prophecy.

Administrations from the Lord Jesus Christ

"And he [Jesus] gave some apostles; and some prophets; and some evangelists; and some pastors, and teachers." Ephesians 4:11 AMP.

Jesus Christ set up five different administrators in his church, with one being the prophet. An administrator is defined as managing and being responsible for the running of a business or organization, in this case, Jesus' church. The Strong's Greek dictionary defines it as service, ministry, especially of those who execute the commands of the Lord.

Jesus only gives some this administrative work, meaning all aren't qualified or called to do it. Therefore, all prophets, while similar, are different. Here's what I have found.

Kinds of Prophets:

The Occasional "Prophet"

This person prophesies on occasion as the Holy Spirit leads. Their prophecies are more of a personal nature for the encouragement and edification of individual saints. We all can prophesy, but only as the Spirit gives us utterance, but this doesn't happen all the time to all of us **(Joel 2:28).** This is the gift of prophecy where the Spirit that's activated as the Spirit wills. An example of prophecy would be: "Be encouraged. Your daughter with cancer will be healed by the end of this month."

The Operational Prophet

This Prophet, like the first, except they prophesy all the time. That is the office of the Prophet. It's their God-given function and identity in the body of Christ. Prophets are speakers on God's behalf, giving encouragement, edification, warnings, etc., to each member of the body. An example of prophecy is "God will bless you in this specific area if you do this or that.

The Administrative Prophet

This Prophet has a greater responsibility. Along with the abilities of the first two, they watch over the other prophets and keep them in line **(1 Corinthians 14:29-33).** The administrative prophet helps oversee the church and the direction it's going. These prophets hear the heart of God and express how He feels. The administrative prophet helps prepare God's people for trials and tribulations on a grand scale. When there's sin in the church, and nothing is being done about it, this prophet is the one to expose it. He'll call for repentance and restoration and, in the worst case, remove such people **(Jeremiah 1:9-10).**

Administrative prophets are similar to the major prophets of Israel, who were committed to God's Will in the face of adversity from others. There were major and minor prophets in the bible, but these labels did not imply that one set of prophets was more important. Length of work is the main determining factor when deciding whether a prophet is major or minor. Both labels are used strictly within the Old Testament. The terms major and minor Prophets are simply a way to divide the Old Testament prophetic books. The major prophets are much longer in length of work and fewer in number, and the minor prophets are shorter in the length of work and greater in number. The major Prophets are Isaiah, Jeremiah, Lamentations, Ezekiel, and Daniel. The minor prophets are Hosea, Joel, Obadiah, Jonah, Micah, Nahum, Habakkuk, Zephaniah, Haggai, Zechariah, and Malachi.

The administrative prophet usually carries out an extended length of work. Prophets do not exist for their own glory but for the glory of God. The Hebrew word for prophet is Nebi, derived from the verb action, "to bubble forth" like a fountain. Prophets authoritatively speak on God's behalf and never on their own authority. They do not share their own opinions while prophesying either. They only share the message as God instructs them. Their role is to make God's Will known, as well as His holiness.

Prophecy is the Holy Spirit

The Holy Spirit is the only reason why prophets can prophesy. Holy Spirit is the Spirit of God which reveals all truth and lives inside of the believer. The Holy Spirit is omnipresent (everywhere at once) and omniscient (all-knowing). The Holy Spirit is the **third person of the triune Godhead** (Matthew 28:19; 2 Corinthians 13:14). The Spirit is not an impersonal "it" or simply an influence but a personal being just as the Father and the Son. He is divine and has intelligence (1 Corinthians 2:10-11), emotions (Ephesians 4:30), and a will (1 Corinthians 2:11). Referring to the Holy Spirit, Yeshua affirmed in John 16:8 NIV, "When he comes, he will convict the world about sin, righteousness, and judgment."

The Holy Spirit is referred to as oil, fire, wind, a river, and wine in the Bible, but that does not take away from Him being the Spirit of God. God is powerful and can transition into anything needed to get our attention. Most importantly, the Holy Spirit is a gift poured out and given liberally to those who ask (Acts 2:17).

The Bible says that He comes upon us, moves on us, falls on us, anoints us, baptizes us, fills us, dwells in us, and flows out of us. The Holy Spirit also has intentions, shows willfulness and discretion, loves, communicates, testifies, teaches, and prays (Nehemiah 9:20; John 15:26; Acts 13:2; Romans 8:26,27; 15:30; 1Corinthians 12:11).

Holy Spirit:

Is our helper

Sanctifies us

Makes us more like Christ

Helps us to do the Father's will

Gifts us for ministry

Imparts love

Gives us hopes

Teaches and gives us insight

Guides our prayers

Uses us for evangelism to create disciples

— Chapter 2 —

AM I A PROPHET?

The Gift vs. The Office

The gift of prophecy is for all who desire to prophesy, and the Holy Spirit allows it. The office of a prophet is a calling or identity by God, whether one claims it or not. The prophet is one of the five-fold ministry titles of Jesus/Yeshua detailed in **Ephesians 4:11-12**.

> To be a Prophet is a calling or identity of someone who prophesies.
>
> One who ministers in prophecy is gifted and not called to be a prophet.

The Bible tells us in **1 Corinthians 14:31 NIV, "For you can all prophesy in turn so that everyone may be instructed and encouraged."**

Apostle Paul encourages the Corinthians to desire the gift of prophecy above any other gifts. He explains why it is used in the church above the use of the gift of tongues if nobody is available to interpret. Prophecy benefits everyone, but praying in tongues with nobody to interpret benefits only the speaker. Only two or three tongues-speakers should contribute to any service, and only then one at a time and followed by interpreters. The same applies to prophecy and the gift of discerning spirits. Orderliness and building up the church are guiding principles for worship meetings.

The Gift:

Prophecy is one of the gifts given by the Holy Spirit, and it is Not a calling or title. Prophecy is the "message" God releases through the Holy Spirit to be delivered to His people. The message and the Holy Spirit are the gifts. Anyone can prophesy if they possess the Holy Spirit, are open to Him, and are willing to be used. The gift of prophecy is freely given to believers just as the Fruits of the Holy Spirit. **It is the Holy Spirit that is activated on the inside of God's people that allows the message or prophecy to come forward.** How do you get this gift? Ask God for it (1 Corinthians 14:1, 39). The gift of prophecy is simply the manifestation of the Holy Spirit using a willing vessel as He chooses.

The Manifestation & Gifts of The Holy Spirit:

Wisdom

Knowledge

Faith

Healing

Power to perform miracles

Prophecy

Distinguishing between spirits

Speaking in different kinds of tongues

Interpretation of tongues

The Holy Spirit shows Himself in nine different ways through *every* man as He wills. One of which is prophecy. God anoints the prophet to prophesy, but prophecy will only come through the Holy Spirit. Prophecy is the message that is the gift. The only difference is who delivers the message. Prophecy is a supernatural utterance in a known tongue that edifies, encourages, and comforts the church. **1 Corinthians 12:4,10 NIV; 1 Corinthians 14:3-5 NIV.**

Prophesy: *Verb*

"to utter by or as if by divine inspiration; to predict with assurance or the revelation of divine knowledge."

The Holy Spirit leads and guides all prophecy. Therefore, the Holy Spirit should not be quenched, or He will become grieved. We hinder the Holy Spirit from moving when we lie, use negative speech, don't control our emotions, fall into deception or drunkenness, steal, etc. In other words, we stop the move of the Holy Spirit inside us when we disobey the Lord then the Holy Spirit becomes saddened. Holy Spirit is activated through obedience to God, the Fruits of the Spirit, forgiveness, pure speech, and God's love. We display God's love when we obey God's commands. We are all meant to pursue the God type of love (agape) **1 Corinthians 13: 4-8 NIV**, be zealous in the gift of prophecy and speak prophetic words of edification, exhortation, and comfort to build others up. We all get to unwrap the gift of prophecy, and then we get to give it away to others. Freely we have received; freely we can give!

GIFT OF PROPHECY

It's a gift of the Holy Spirit.

Every believer is encouraged to prophesy.

It's for **e**dification, **e**xhortation, and **c**omfort.

The prophetic utterance is a gift.

The gift is ministry.

The gift is for life.

The gift is the message of the Holy Spirit.

Those with prophetic gifts will express them in different ways, such as song, dance, etc. God has the final say in the way one operates. We also prophesy according to our Faith. Faith comes by hearing when we hear God's living word. **Romans 10:17 NIV** says, "faith comes by hearing, and hearing by the word of God." This scripture is not only present tense, but it also means the "Word" of God. It was translated from the Greek word *rhema, which* means "that which is or has been uttered by the living voice." The scriptures tell us that the word of God is God Himself.

In other words, we are graced with the gift and must prophesy according to our level of faith or knowledge of God's word. **Romans 12:6 NIV.**

Even if our faith is that of a mustard seed, we can speak to mountains to move them. **1 Corinthians 14:30-31** declares all of us can prophesy, but prophecies must be given one at a time decently and in order.

THE OFFICE:

The office of the prophet is a governmental position among the church or body of Christ. The Prophet is God's representative or ambassador by communicating God's word to His people.

Numbers 12:6 NIV, "And he said, Hear now my words: If there be a prophet among you, I the LORD will make myself known unto him in a vision, and will speak unto him in a dream."

The office of the prophet is divinely appointed and affirmed by God. God predestines and anoints the prophet for their calling. The prophet is commissioned to speak God's word and train the body of Christ to do the work of God's Kingdom. The prophet is also required to do the will of God and operate in love so the Holy Spirit can remain active in one's life.

The prophet's job isn't just to prophesy over individuals but to teach the church how to hear the voice of God more clearly. Another function of their calling is to point others to God and show them the way. Prophets may lead the way by releasing words that indicate timing to the church's leadership of where they are going and how to stay on track. Some prophets tend to be very straightforward in their approach to giving divine direction, re-direction, correction, and seeing into the spiritual realms where others cannot.

The prophet should love God's people and His church with the love of God. Therefore, the prophet's delivery should never be judgmental or critical but firm and direct. Do not misunderstand when I use the word judgment because God does send words of judgement through His prophets. The prophet should always deliver God's words of judgement in love. The prophet's desire should be to push the believers to be all God has called them to be.

OFFICE OF A PROPHET

It's a gift from the Godhead.

God chooses the person for the office; it's not our choice.

The office is to train, equip, direct, correct, warn, and govern God's people.

The prophet is a gift to the body of Christ.

The prophet is a governing official that is part of the five-fold ministry.

The calling of the prophet is for life.

How do I know if I am a prophet?

God will reveal it to you.

God has called you to hear the whispers of what is in His heart and to learn what His intention is, then pass it on to others. *"No one can come to me unless the Father who sent me draws them, and I will raise them up at the last day. It is written in the Prophets: 'They will all be taught by God. Everyone who has heard the Father and learned from him comes to me." John 6:44-45 NIV.*

God will draw you into Himself.

God has placed His desires within you because He is drawing you toward your purpose and destiny. *"Take delight in the Lord, and he will give you the desires of your heart." Psalm 37:4 NIV*

God has given you knowledge in prayer that you could not have known naturally.

Prophetic prayer is powerful because you are praying according to God's purposes. As 1 John 5:14-15 NIV states, *'This is the confidence we have in approaching God: that if we ask anything according to his will, he hears us. And if we know that he hears us—whatever we ask—we know that we have what we asked of him."*

You have been through a trial concerning your calling.

A pattern we see in scripture is that someone who has a ministry calling goes through a trial, failure, or what we call a 'wilderness experience' where it seems the world is against them. So, if you have had difficulties with others after you released what God revealed to you, or you have felt alone, be encouraged! That may be a sign you are chosen for the calling. Don't let the enemy hook you to an experience through hurt or disappointment. Remember, Proverbs 4:23 NIV declares, "Above all else, guard your heart, for everything you do flows from it." Do whatever it takes to obey God and forgive others and yourself. Keep your heart pure and hands clean.

Who is a Prophet?

Deuteronomy 18:18 NIV, "I will raise them up a Prophet from among their brethren, like unto thee, and will put my words in his mouth; and he shall speak unto them all that I shall command him."

A prophet reveals Jesus Christ through prophecies and revelations and gives God's commandments to the people. A prophet provides the church with direction. God has outpoured His Spirit, as prophesied by

Joel. That is the reason we have more prophets than in the early times. Since a prophet is God's voice, there are consequences for ignoring prophets. A prophet is someone chosen by God to speak for God. Their job is to impart His message accurately. They all have in common a heart for God, an anointing to hear from Him, and the faithfulness to impart His message to others.

> *"For prophecy never had its origin in the human will, but prophets, though human, spoke from God as they were carried along by the Holy Spirit." (2 Peter 1:21 NIV).*

In some ways, a prophet is an advocate or mediator between God and a group of people. God doesn't always speak directly to only one group of people. For instance, God gave the prophet Jonah a message for the Assyrians, an enemy of Israel at the time (**Jonah 4:6-9 NIV**). The prophet Daniel carried a dispatch for the Babylonians about their imminent demise via the hand of the Medes and Persians (**Daniel 5:25-28 NIV**). However, sometimes God uses prophets to speak to His people. For instance, God commanded Jeremiah to speak against Israel's idolatrous ways. (**Jeremiah 7 NIV**).

The Prophet:

1. Has a special relationship with God.

God sets His prophets apart for Himself in a way not reserved for others. Just like the priests of old, the prophet is called to minister to God first and then to the people. As a result, prophets have a very close relationship with God and a deep desire for more of Him.

2. Shares special moments of intimacy with God.

Jesus, described as a prophet by those who met Him, spent long hours alone with His Father. Jesus often spent long hours before essential events in His ministry, such as the calling of His disciples and the garden of Gethsemane. In the case of Ezekiel, he was so overwhelmed by his encounter with God's throne that he was rendered exhausted and mute for days afterward.

In the same way, modern-day prophets will experience intimate moments with God.

3. Receives a download of power from the Holy Spirit.

Some prophets received an injection of power from God at the inauguration of their ministry. Jesus, for example, was baptized by John the Baptist, then the Holy Spirit came down "like a dove" and anointed Him for His ministry. **(Luke 3:22 NIV).**

4. Receives a specific word from God Himself that one is called to the office.

God told Jeremiah and Isaiah specifically that He had called them to the office of the prophet. Isaiah saw a vision of God's throne in heaven, and a flaming creature with six wings touched his lips with burning coal. The Lord asked who would speak for Him, and Isaiah responded he would. So, God told him to "go and give the people His message." (Isaiah 6:9 NIV).

Jeremiah's call was even more explicit: The word of the Lord came to me, saying, "Before I formed you in the womb I knew you, before you were born I set you apart; I appointed you as a prophet to the nations." **(Jeremiah 1:4-5 NIV).**

5. Practice obedience.

Prophets may sometimes find God asking them to do or say things they don't understand at first. In such situations, obedience is the key! God trains His prophets to be obedient and to trust Him. Complete understanding may come later if that is the Lord's will. Prophets just need to obey. Jesus showed the importance of obedience. **"Very truly I tell you, the Son can do nothing by himself; he can do only what he sees his Father doing, because whatever the Father does the Son also does." (John 5:19 NIV).**

6. Has a strong sense of justice.

Prophets hate to see people suffering, particularly the vulnerable, who cannot defend themselves. That may lead the prophet to speak out about unjust situations, but they sometimes become judgmental if they are not careful. Balance the desire for justice with a deep understanding of God's love for the world.

7. Receives vision of Heaven.

God sometimes shows the prophet visions of heaven to impress upon the prophet the true reality of who He is. God may also give such visions to those prophets who are called Seers. Seers can literally see into heaven. They may also see things in the spirit that others can't see.

8. May have many dreams from God.

Some prophets dream instead of having visions. These dreams tend to be detailed and occasionally complex. The key that distinguishes dreams from God is that there is clarity to them not found in an ordinary dream. More importantly, dreams take time to interpret and fully understand.

9. May see biblical symbols in everyday life.

Prophets may see signs which reveal what God is about to do.

10. Aim for God's standard of righteousness and holiness.

Prophets don't just want to "preach God's word;" they want to live it too! "Seek first his kingdom *and his righteousness*" (**Matthew 6:33 NIV**).

11. Is motivated to learn more about prophecy.

Prophets also want to go *deeper*. Deeper into God and deeper into His gifts so that they can become more effective in their calling.

12. Has an ongoing ministry.

The prophet doesn't just speak once. They have a gift from the Holy Spirit, which is to benefit others, not just themselves.
That implies the sharing of prophecy is an ongoing, continuous ministry.

13. Feel set apart and may feel lonely.

Being called to be a prophet isn't glamorous. Prophets are sometimes misunderstood. It can be exciting to share prophecies, but it can sometimes be very lonely. Isaiah's life is an example. He prophesied many years to a people who would not listen to the message!

14. Will not be recognized as a prophet.

Recognition comes first from God Himself and then from those assigned to see.

— Chapter 3 —

ACTIVATION OF THE PROPHET

I remember having so many questions about a prophet when I was younger. Then once I got married, my wife had a list of questions about a prophet as well. At this point, I'm convinced no one knows every detail about the prophet unless God reveals it to them. I am honored that God would reveal such mysteries to me. For years I thought I knew what it was to be a prophet, but I only saw a glimpse until the Lord challenged me to write this book. Things that seemed so basic were really another level of activation. The deeper we go with God, the more He reveals. It wasn't until the Lord blessed me with seven children who are prophets that I wanted to go deeper to teach them. I wanted them to be prepared to be used by God and know how to war against Satan when he sets up traps. I did not want our children to be blindsided as my wife and I was when we started walking in our calling. I'm grateful God gave me the insight to teach others as well. Once you discover you are a prophet, how do you activate the office? Is there such a thing as "activating the office?" The short answer is Yes and No. The long answer is God is the only one who can activate His prophets, but we, as prophets, must obey His commands to flow how God created us. As I stated before, prophets cannot prophesy without the Spirit of God, which is the Holy Spirit. Holy Spirit leads and guides the prophets, just as He does God's people. The prophet gets assignments, instructions, directions, interpretations, revelations, and wisdom from the Holy Spirit. Holy Spirit is the Spirit of truth and the gift of prophecy. Therefore, no prophet can speak on God's behalf without the Holy Spirit.

1 Corinthians 12:1-11 NIV, "Now about the gifts of the Spirit, brothers, and sisters, I do not want you to be uninformed. You know that when you were pagans, somehow or other you were influenced and led astray to mute idols. Therefore, I want you to know that no one who is speaking by the Spirit of God says, "Jesus be cursed," and no one can say, "Jesus is Lord," except by the Holy Spirit. There are different kinds of gifts, but the same Spirit distributes them. There are different kinds of service, but the same Lord. There are different kinds of working, but in all of them and in everyone it is the same God at work. Now to each one the manifestation of the Spirit is given for the common good. To one there is given through the Spirit a message of wisdom, to another a message of knowledge by means of the same Spirit, to another faith by the same Spirit, to another gifts of healing by that one Spirit, to another miraculous powers, to another prophecy, to another distinguishing between spirits, to another speaking in different kinds of tongues, and to still another the interpretation of tongues. All these are the work of one and the same Spirit, and he distributes them to each one, just as he determines."

If one comes as a prophet but do not have the Holy Spirit, they are a false prophet because the Truth is not in them. The only way you can tell the fake from the real prophet is through prayer. Why? Because God is the revealer of truth. Go to God in prayer, and He will expose the truth, so we do not fall prey to Satan's schemes. Satan uses the false prophet to turn the people away from God. Therefore, prayer keeps the righteous in the know. Prayer is a weapon against darkness and an intimate interaction or communication with God, most frequently through a spontaneous, unorganized form of petitioning and gratitude. Prayer should be the prophet's first language.

Matthew 7:15 NIV, "Beware of false prophets, which come to you in sheep's clothing, but inwardly they are ravening wolves."

1 John 4:1 ESV, "Beloved, do not believe every spirit, but test the spirits to see whether they are from God, for many false prophets have gone out into the world."

The prophet must also walk, speak, think, and breathe in God's love to be activated. If God is love, then that wraps us back around to understanding that God activates the prophet. God created us and knew us before we were formed in the womb. Therefore, He knows the appointed time He chose to activate the prophet for their ministry just as He did with Jesus.

God's Love:

1 Corinthians 13:2 NIV, "If I have the gift of prophecy and can fathom all mysteries and all knowledge, and if I have a faith that can move mountains, but do not have love, I am nothing.

1 Corinthians 13:4-10 NIV, "Love is patient, love is kind. It does not envy, it does not boast, it is not proud. It does not dishonor others, it is not self-seeking, it is not easily angered, it keeps no record of wrongs. Love does not delight in evil but rejoices with the truth. It always protects, always trusts, always hopes, always perseveres. Love never fails. But where there are prophecies, they will cease; where there are tongues, they will be stilled; where there is knowledge, it will pass away. For we know in part and we prophesy in part, but when completeness comes, what is in part disappears."

1 Corinthians 13:13 NIV, "And now these three remain: faith, hope and love. But the greatest of these is love."

1 Corinthians 14:1 NIV, "Follow the way of love and eagerly desire gifts of the Spirit, especially prophecy."

Prioritize the Prophetic:

"Pursue love, and desire spiritual gifts, but especially that you may prophesy." We are to pursue the manifestation of all these gifts in our lives, but we are to go after learning to prophesy above all others. God would never tell us to desire something He did not want us to have. **Understand the Nature of the New Testament Prophet:** *"And it shall come to pass in the last days, says God, that I will pour out my Spirit on all people; your son and your daughters shall prophesy, your young men will see visions, your old men will dream dreams. (Acts 2:17 NIV).* Not only will it manifest through us all, but the nature of the prophetic is now primarily to encourage. Yes, those called to the office of a prophet may rebuke and correct, but that is not the sole purpose of the prophetic.

Believe Your Words Are Powerful:

"The tongue has the power of life and death, and those who love it will eat its fruit. (Proverbs 18:21 NIV). "Let no corrupt word proceed out of your mouth, but what is good for necessary edification, that it may impart grace to the hearers." (Ephesians 4:29 NIV). "The words that I speak to you are spirit, and they are life." (John 6:63 NIV.) When we understand and believe our words are not just information but life and grace to the hearers, then we are ready for great prophetic ministry. Our assignment is not to convince people of what we are saying but to believe our words impart life. Believing takes the prophetic to another level.

Be An Encourager:

Prophets **ARE** encouragers looking for and identifying the greatness in people because they know what it's like to be rejected and abandoned. Plus, love will push the prophet to encourage even when they do not want to.

Understand Your Identity:

The most vital prophetic words identify who God calls us to be because Satan wants us to think less of ourselves, so we do not carry out our purpose. Once we understand who we are, the words we release over others, cities, nations, and ourselves will become more influential.

— Chapter 4 —

PRINCIPLES OF THE OFFICE

There is a right way and a wrong way to do things, especially regarding a job or calling. Sometimes there is a way and a "better" way if that makes sense. Time is valuable, so if you can come up with the correct outcome in a shorter time, it's a win across the board. No one can teach the prophet "how to be" a prophet except God because He created the prophet for Himself. Although, one can steer you in the right direction to understand the calling. There is much to learn as a prophet, and all prophets deliver differently. Prophets can even make a mess of a thing while trying to walk in their calling if they do not rely on Holy Spirit. It is easy to step out of bounds and end up in witchcraft if one is not careful. The prophet can be led by a spirit, but not the Holy Spirit, which would get them in trouble with God. Hence why prayer, the word of God, and a relationship with God are the fundamentals of a prophet's life. Here are some principles or guidelines to live by as a prophet.

A prophet's lifestyle begins with an intimate relationship with God. God wants to commune with us and share what is on His heart. Prophets should always keep their ears to God's mouth, waiting for the following instructions. Further, if we cannot receive or discern His word for ourselves, how can we expect to have it for others? Having a close relationship with God in which we receive prophetic guidance (instruction from the Holy Spirit) or 'hear and obey'—is essential to unlocking the mysteries of the supernatural. Prophets live in accordance with the word of God (which is God Himself).

Walking in the prophetic is to have clear foresight and insight into what is happening in the realm of the spiritual world. Seeing ahead of what will ultimately occur in one's life and others is truly a gift from God. Knowing the thoughts of God is required to stay within His perfect will. The prophetic is not always favorable among the people because most do not like correction. But who are you going to please, man or God? God tests the prophet with obedience so they can become stronger to defeat Satan. The story of the young prophet and the old prophet in the Bible is a classic to display the importance of obedience. **(I Kings 13:1-26 NIV)**. God gave the young prophet instructions to follow, but he disobeyed God to please the old prophet, who gave him a false prophetic word. God got angry and allowed an animal to kill the young prophet. Then God told the old prophet to clean up the young prophet's body. The moral of the story, obey God at all costs, no matter if "they" seem more experienced in God than you. God does not care about age, when we accepted salvation, or how long we have been in the "church." He wants us to love Him by obeying His commands. We must do and say as the Holy Spirit leads. God will pour out according to your level of understanding, your relationship with Him, and your faith.

We must deny ourselves.

The Lord wants us to align our desires with His even in conflict. We can not do anything without God. Therefore, deny fears, inabilities, and sinful temptations by the power of the Holy Spirit. We can do all things through Christ, who strengthens us.

We must take up our cross daily.

Jesus encourages us to carry forth His cross, which is His agenda and mission. We are to be the salt of the earth or virtuous, spread the Good News or life of Yeshua, and be Christ's ambassadors to the world. We should love the unlovable, forgive the ones who don't deserve forgiveness, extend grace, and attempt to bring reconciliation through Christ. That is His cross.

We must follow Him.

Jesus is our leader, and every day we need to mimic the Savior. Although it won't always be easy, it's not impossible. Culture, tradition, religion, and Satan will work against us. Some in the church will still want to write more rules, but following Jesus will always be best. Following Yeshua is part of being a disciple. In fact, that is discipleship.

The prophet & prophecy should always point the people to God.

> *Revelation 19:10 NIV, "And I fell at his feet to worship him. But he said to me, "See that you do not do that! I am your fellow servant, and of your brethren who have the testimony of Jesus. Worship God! For the testimony of Jesus is the spirit of prophecy."*

The true Spirit of prophecy always shows itself in bearing witness to Jesus. Any teaching of prophecy that takes our minds and hearts away from God is not being adequately communicated, and it is the antichrist. That means that prophecy, at its very core, is designed to unfold the beauty and loveliness of our Lord and Savior, Jesus Christ. Prophets should never steal glory from God. Prophets are only who they are because of God.

Laws & Principles of the Prophetic Ministry

Principle 1: The Bible is its own interpreter. We do not have to argue the word of God. Release the word and allow the Holy Spirit to do the rest.

Principle 2: Prophecy is always Christ-Centered, and every interpretation must reveal Yeshua Hamashiach. True prophecy brings God glory.

Principle 3: When prophecies are repeated, the repetition contains an explanation with added information. This process pulls one closer to promise and gives a deeper understanding. God wants to build us up so we can finally see the whole picture He prepared for us.

Only say what God says.

Don't allow people to push you to channel in the spirit without the leading of the Holy Spirit. Prophets can tap into a demonic realm of "familiar spirits" sent out to monitor and report information to Satan concerning us. Satan is not omnipresent, so he needs spies/ demons to cover territory on his behalf. When prophesying outside of the Holy Spirit, it is considered witchcraft because it violates the laws of God. False prophets release words, not from God but messages from demons waiting to distract us. There are also words to keep us from going forward in God's will.

The false prophet was never anointed or given access from God to prophesy. Hence why demonic spirits lead them to speak into someone's life. Holy Spirit will reveal to the prophet whatever God wants them to know, so there is no need to make things happen. Demonic spirits control the false prophet and target God's people, so they will forfeit blessings and abort their purpose. Check the source of the prophecy no matter if they go to "church" or not. Many unbelievers go to church as well. If they do not confess Jesus/ Yeshua is Lord, they are unbelievers, and the Spirit of truth is not in them.

> *"We also have the prophetic message as something completely reliable, and you will do well to pay attention to it, as to a light shining in a dark place, until the day dawns and the morning star rises in your hearts. Above all, you must understand that no prophecy of Scripture came about by the prophet's own interpretation of things. For prophecy never had its origin in the human will, but prophets, though human, spoke from God as they were carried along by the Holy Spirit." (2 Peter 1:19-21 NIV).*

Consequences for prophesying falsely.

> *Revelations 19:20 NIV, "But the beast was captured, and with it the false prophet who had performed the signs on its behalf. With these signs he had deluded those who had received the mark of the beast and worshiped its image. The two of them were thrown alive into the fiery lake of burning sulfur."*

God is not pleased when we use His name in vain and mislead His people. Saying God said a thing, but He did not is using God's name in vain, not just swearing by His name. God's name is sacred, and it should be honored. Demons tremble at His great name, which should make us respect Yeshua's name even more.

Watch your mouth!

> *Proverbs 18:21 KJV, "Death and life are in the power of the tongue: and they that love it shall eat the fruit thereof."*

Our words are powerful because God gave us power and dominion. Our power comes with the Holy Spirit, which is the Spirit of God. Therefore, we must live a holy and consecrated life so that Holy Spirit can move freely within and through us. We can not speak death or curses unless God authorizes it, or we fall into witchcraft. Witchcraft is rebellion against God's word through manipulation and control. When we rebel against God, Satan has control of us, and the truth is not in us. God will judge us for every idle or unauthorized word we speak. God commands us to be Holy, which includes our speech because He is holy.

Judge Every Prophetic Word.

Just because someone says or declares to you that they are a prophet does not mean they are. Satan also sends people to distract us and lead us astray. Satan is the father of lies. Therefore, make sure Satan is not in the middle regarding receiving direction. Judge every word against the Holy Spirit to see if it's from God. Simply pray and ask God what to do and reveal deeper details. The Holy Spirit will respond with directions or instructions. Beware of the false prophets! *Deuteronomy 18:22 "If what a prophet proclaims in the name of the LORD does not take place or come true, that is a message the LORD has not spoken. That prophet has spoken presumptuously, so do not be alarmed."*

Knowing The Difference Between Familiar/Divination Spirits and A Prophetic Word.

There are demonic spirits that give limited insight into your future using things familiar to you or something you desire to gain credibility; these are spirits of divination or familiar spirits. Those who operate in the spirit of divination are oracles (spokespeople) for a demonic spirit. Oracles know things about you from familiar spirits that use them as channels to speak their manipulation. These demonic spirits communicate to the oracle your issues, thus giving them insight regarding what's going on in your life. The oracles then begin to speak your issues to you, causing you to listen and think that this can only be the Lord.

The spirits will give you a small portion of the truth to pull you in, and then they twist the insight with a lie to get you off track with your purpose. Remember, they have joined forces with Satan; therefore, their job is to steal, kill, and destroy. Many of these oracles, psychics, tarot card readers, etc., are even in the church operating because some can't judge the truth from the fake. There is a very thin line between prophecy and witchcraft.

> *Acts 16:16–18 ESV, "As we were going to the place of prayer, we were met by a slave girl who had a spirit of divination and brought her owners much gain by fortune-telling. She followed Paul and us, crying out, "These men are servants of the Most High God, who proclaim to you the way of salvation." And this she kept doing for many days. Paul, having become greatly annoyed, turned and said to the spirit, "I command you in the name of Jesus Christ to come out of her." And it came out that very hour."*

This girl was possessed by a familiar spirit. Notice that what she was saying was true! There was no error in what she said about Paul and the other men. That is one way the devil draws people in -by presenting something true initially. Satan is an angel who was once in heaven, so he knows some things about us. He does not know all as God does, but he will use the portion he has to his advantage.

Some who have genuine prophetic gifts can also miss God when they operate in emotion and ambition, are sensitive to relationships, and move based on their knowledge of something, etc. Those serving in the prophetic must spend time with God in prayer to hear clearly from Holy Spirit. There will be times to release the word and other times to pray on behalf of that situation. We will know if the word was from God if it happens, but if it does not, the word was not from God.

> *Jeremiah 23:26 NIV declares, "How long shall this be in the heart of the prophets that prophesy lies? Yea, they are prophets of the deceit of their own heart."*

Order.

God will direct you, and open the door for you to speak, yet in order. God will bring you before the person or people He wants you to talk to. These people will often not have any spiritual oversight; thus, God has established them as part of your territory. There must be accountability and order; without it would cause complete chaos. God does not work in darkness; neither does He operate out of order. If you have a prophetic word for someone inside a church you do not belong to, you should ask the leader for permission first, only out of courtesy. The exception to this is when leadership is in overt sin, and a word of correction must come forward.

Pride and ambition often cause some with prophetic gifts to operate illegally, causing confusion in the ranks of God's people.

Prophetic Words Are Not To Lead You.

A prophetic word will be either confirmation or a warning. The dictionary describes prophecy as a prediction or something that could possibly happen. When prophecy comes from God, it's guaranteed to happen in its timing because God can not lie. Prophecy does have a set time to reveal itself because the process may need to take place within the individual. Some prophecies come with instructions and only happen based on the individual's obedience. Otherwise, there will be a hold until one obeys.

Not For Pay!

Prophetic words are not for sale, nor are those who operate in this gift for hire. If God has a word, then He has a word, and no amount of money can be given to give that word or withhold that word. Prophecy belongs to God because they are His words, and they do not belong to the prophet. How can one charge for something that does not belong to them?? I have seen too often prophets charge the people to release prophecy. Prophets cannot exchange or barter the word of God for influence either. Neither should prophets try to speak a favorable word to someone because of their title or position. Prophets must say whatever God instructs, whether a person is rich or poor, prestigious or lowly, or has a title. Prophetic words must be given purely because God says so and not because of anything else.

A Not So Pleasant Prophetic Word.

Contrary to popular practices and opinions, not all prophetic words are favorable. There are probably more non-favorable prophetic words that God wants His servants to give than favorable ones because of the lukewarm condition of today's church. Most people don't want to hear prophetic words that are not about blessings, financial increases, etc. They are quick to receive the words of blessings but not correction. Yet God sends this kind of prophetic word for the benefit and growth of His people.

So, what should a person do when they receive a prophetic word that is unfavorable? Should they get mad at the vessel that delivered the word? Should they cast it down as a word from the enemy? Should they ignore it, declaring that they are a child of the King? Should they seek someone to give them a favorable prophetic word that would counter the non-favorable prophetic word given to them? None of these things are the correct response. Many in the Body of Christ do not have on their Belts of Truth, which would give them the ability to do an honest self-examination, thus giving them the ability to receive a non-favorable prophetic word in humility. Some non-favorable prophetic words are meant to warn us of what's coming, and others are to cause us to repent and turn from certain behavior, etc.

The question again is, "what should a person do when they are given a non-favorable prophetic word?" Establish if it's an accurate word from the Lord, then repent from the sins or actions that caused this word to come to you. You should seek the Lord's face to ask Him for grace and mercy to go through deliverance. King Hezekiah was delivered a not so favorable prophetic word in **II Kings 20:1-6 NIV.** The prophet told him to set his house in order because he would die. Hezekiah's response was not denial, neither did he seek another prophet to counter that unfavorable word spoken to him; rather, he sought God's face in prayer and wept, which was a sign of repentance. That caused God to add to his life 15 more years. Those called to give difficult prophetic words should not run from it like prophet Jonah, and neither should those who are recipients of them do nothing about them. Be bold to speak the word of the Lord and be wise in seeking the Lord when you have received an unfavorable word.

— Chapter 5 —

THE ANOINTING & THE MANTLE

The difference between mantles and anointing: **The anointing stays with the prophet, but the mantle remains with the mission**. Sometimes people are anointed as a prophet, but they have yet to receive the mantle to walk in the office. Until they receive their mantle, they have no leadership role as a prophet.

God's **mantle is His character and glory. The** nature and glory of God is developed in us by an intimate relationship with God called **anointing**. A mantle in the natural is a cloak or outer garment to cover the body. A mantle is used symbolically in the Bible as the righteous call and covering of God in fulfilling our destinies. If we are under the guidance and direction of the Holy Spirit, then we will be in the perfect will of the Father.

What is a mantle?

The Hebrew word for mantle is 'addereth. The definition is glory; clock; splendor; magnificence. Cloak made of fur or fine material; robe.

Another Hebrew word for mantle is me'il. The definition is clock or robe and is frequently known as the "robe of the ephod" (Exodus 28:6-14), a fine linen tunic. It was worn not only by priests but by kings, prophets, and rich men. The tunic was the "little coat" that Samuel's mother brought to him yearly to Shiloh, a miniature official priestly robe.

The Ephod

"Make the ephod of gold, and of blue, purple and scarlet yarn, and of finely twisted linen—the work of skilled hands. It is to have two shoulder pieces attached to two of its corners, so it can be fastened. Its skillfully woven waistband is to be like it—of one piece with the ephod and made with gold, and with blue, purple and scarlet yarn, and with finely twisted linen. "Take two onyx stones and engrave on them the names of the sons of Israel in the order of their birth—six names on one stone and the remaining six on the other. Engrave the names of the sons of Israel on the two stones the way a gem cutter engraves a seal. Then mount the stones in gold filigree settings and fasten them on the shoulder pieces of the ephod as memorial stones for the sons of Israel. Aaron is to bear the names on his shoulders as a memorial before the Lord. Make gold filigree settings and two braided chains of pure gold, like a rope, and attach the chains to the settings." Exodus 28:6-14 NIV.

The mantle is a symbol of authority and position.

What comes with the mantle?

Power

Position

Authority

Protection

Respect

An example of one who naturally walks in a mantle is the president. While they are in this position, they have the protection of the mantle. The president has secret service covering them, and you can't get near him because he has protection. The president has the power to make decisions he couldn't make as a civilian. His position also demands respect. He has the authority to make decisions via executive order whether you approve of it or not. This is the mantle.

Spiritually God gives mantles for us to do the work He assigns. An example would be when David did not kill King Saul when he had a few opportunities to do so because Saul was still the King, and he honored God. Therefore, if David attacked Saul, he would've come against the position and authority of King Saul's God-given mantle. The mantle requires respect and honor. You do not have to like the person or what they do, but you must respect their authority. Prophets are mantled by God also and speak with God's authority. When you come against the Prophet of the Lord, you are resisting God's ordinance and bringing judgment against yourself. Prophets, be bold and courageous because God is with you! is

> *Romans 13:1-7 NKJV, "Let every soul be subject to the governing authorities. For there is no authority except from God, and the authorities that exist are appointed by God. Therefore whoever resists the authority resists the ordinance of God, and those who resist will bring judgment on themselves. For rulers are not a terror to good works, but to evil. Do you want to be unafraid of the authority? Do what is good, and you will have praise from the same. For he is God's minister to you for good. But if you do evil, be afraid; for he does not bear the sword in vain; for he is God's minister, an avenger to execute wrath on him who practices evil. Therefore, you must be subject, not only because of wrath but also for conscience' sake. For because of this you also pay taxes, for they are God's ministers attending continually to this very thing. Render therefore to all their due: taxes to whom taxes are due, customs to whom customs, fear to whom fear, honor to whom honor."*

How will I know what mantle I have?

You don't get to choose your mantle because God is the one who decides which mantle you get. Therefore, the best thing to do is ask God what your mantle is. That's it!

What is the Anointing?

The Hebrew word for anointing is Mashiach, and it means anointed or anointed one.

The word Christos is the Greek word for Messiah, which means anointed. The definition of anointing is to ceremonially confer (grant or bestow (a title, degree, benefit, or right)) a divine position of authority to someone. It's the one who has been granted authority by the Lord. The anointing is sacred. The anointing is the Holy Spirit.

> *"Now it is God who makes both us and you stand firm in Christ. He anointed us, set his seal of ownership on us, and put his Spirit in our hearts as a deposit, guaranteeing what is to come." (2 Corinthians 1:21-22 NIV).*

Saved or unsaved, God will anoint whomever He wants to accomplish a particular purpose. King Saul wore the mantle of King, but David was anointed King before King Saul died. Here's how to consider mantles and anointings. David had the anointing to be King, but Saul had the mantle. Elisha was anointed to be the prophet of the land, but Elijah had the mantle. God chose them all, but the anointing helped David and Elisha to do greater works. You can actually function and operate in an anointing and not have a mantle or title.

Mantle: current position; task; assignment; office; calling; title.

Anointing: divine access; support; blessing; the power of the Holy Spirit.

The anointing teaches us all things, and it comes to us through the anointing given to men and women by the Holy Spirit.

> *"But the anointing which you have received from Him abides in you, and you do not need that anyone teach you; but as the same anointing teaches you concerning all things, and is true, and is not a lie, and just as it has taught you, you will abide in Him." (1 John 2:27 NIV).*

In charismatic circles, the anointing is recognized in powerful healing ministries, powerful sermons, and the working of miracles, but there are also other anointings. There is an anointing for jobs, business, and various callings and gifting. The anointing equips and empowers us to build God's kingdom on earth. This world is part of God's manufacturing process. The most important thing is to find out what you are anointed to do and when to move forward in it.

"You have an anointing from the Holy One, and you know all things." (1 John 2:20 NIV).

Prayer:

Yahweh Elohim,

You knew me from my mother's womb, where you formed and fashioned me with purpose. I pray now, God, that you would show me the anointing and mantle that you have placed upon my life. Show me how to walk in it. Please show me where to go so I can learn how to serve. Position me so that I will be in place when it is time. Grant me the grace to go through my process. Give me a heart of patience so that I may wait for your perfect timing. Give me eyes to see the progression of my mantle and anointings. Guide me by your Holy Spirit on how to steward the anointing in a way that will please you. Let me never take credit or glory for what you have given me. Help me to be a light to this world with this anointing and lead people to You, in Yeshua's name, Amen.

www.ingramcontent.com/pod-product-compliance
Lightning Source LLC
Chambersburg PA
CBHW061327120626
46546CB00007B/2709